MYTH OR LEGEND?

Long before people could read or write, stories were passed on by word of mouth. Every time they were told, they changed a little, with a new character added here and a twist to the plot there. From these ever-changing tales, myths and legends were born.

WHAT IS A MYTH?

In early times, people developed stories to explain local customs and natural phenomena, including how the world and humanity developed. These myths were considered sacred and true. Most include superhuman beings with special powers.

WHAT IS A LEGEND?

A legend is very much like a myth. The difference is that a legend is often based on an event that really happened or a person who really existed in relatively recent times.

ANCIENT EGYPT?

Egypt was originally two countries. Around 5,000 years ago, in about 3000 B.C., they became one. For the next 3,000 years, Egypt was one of the richest and most powerful countries in the world.

THE BANKS OF THE NILE

Most of Egypt was known as the Red Land. This was the hot, dry desert, and few people lived there. Nearly all ancient Egyptians lived in the Black Land, on the banks of the Nile River. Whenever the river flooded, it left a rich, black soil behind, which is how the Black Land got its name.

PYRAMIDS AND PHARAOHS

Egypt is famous for its pyramids, which still stand today. They were tombs for the early rulers, sometimes called pharaohs. Pharaohs were believed to be living gods. Later pharaohs were buried in the rocky hillside or in underground tombs in a place called the Valley of the Kings.

The wedjat eye symbolized the eye of the gods Ra and Horus. According to myth Horus' eye was ripped out but magically grew back. The wedjat eye was seen as a lucky charm.

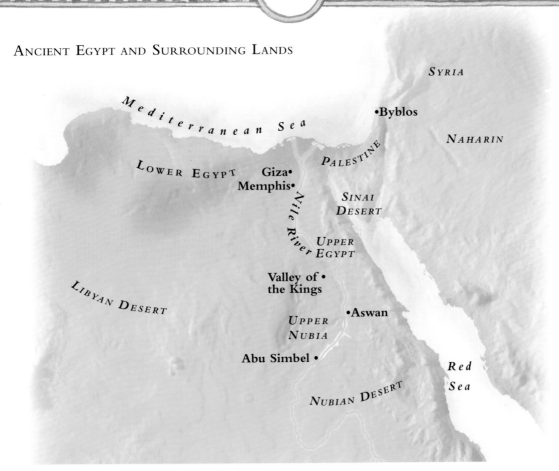

SYRIA

•Byblos

NAHARIN

Mediterranean Sea

PALESTINE

LOWER EGYPT

Giza•
Memphis•

SINAI
DESERT

Nile River

UPPER
EGYPT

Valley of •
the Kings

LIBYAN DESERT

•Aswan

UPPER
NUBIA

Abu Simbel •

*Red
Sea*

NUBIAN DESERT

ANCIENT WRITING

The ancient Egyptians covered their monuments with hieroglyphs, a written language made up of letter and picture symbols. Often these letters were carved into the stone and can still be seen. Many stories were written on papyrus— a sort of paper made from woven reeds. An amazing number of these survive.

CRACKING THE CODE

It was not until the 1820s that experts could decipher what Egyptian hieroglyphs meant. Before then historians relied on written records in other languages, such as ancient Greek. The ancient Greeks kept very accurate written records of the later ancient Egyptian beliefs.

Ancient Egyptian settlements were in the Black Land, on the fertile banks of the Nile River. This was surrounded by deserts—the Red Land.

A MODERN LEGEND

The myths and legends in this book are all from *ancient* Egypt. Another famous Egyptian legend is a modern one—the curse of Tutankhamen. The tomb of Tutankhamen, a boy king in ancient Egypt, was discovered in the Valley of the Kings in 1922. The search was funded by a man called Lord Carnarvon. Rumors spread that the tomb was cursed. According to this modern legend, all the lights went out in Cairo at the moment Lord Carnarvon died, and back in England his dog died, too.

Stories from Ancient Egypt

Ancient Egyptian myths and legends are made up of many different beliefs. Each town and city worshiped its own gods and goddesses. The popularity of some gods spread, and later the stories of these gods merged to form the ones we know in ancient Egyptian mythology.

One Role, Many Gods

One effect of different ancient Egyptians worshiping different gods was that many gods in Egypt had the same duties. For example, there were many sun gods. Each god was worshiped by a different set of people. None of these groups believed in all the gods. Later Ra became known as the sun god, and all the other sun gods were simply said to be manifestations of Ra. The many gods had fused into one.

On the Move

Trade must have played a large part in the spreading of myths and legends. As people from different parts of Egypt traveled across the Black Land selling goods, they probably shared their stories and beliefs. People began to learn of different gods, goddesses, myths, and legends and absorbed them into their own beliefs.

The Creation

Even something as important as the creation of the earth and its people was told in many different versions. One of the earliest, which came from the city of Heliopolis, said that Atum was the creator. Later, when Ra became the most powerful of all ancient Egyptian gods, he became the creator and– in this form–was referred to as Ra-Atum.

Familiar Names

Hundreds of gods and goddesses were worshiped in ancient Egypt. Here is a list of some of the more important ones.

RA (sometimes RE) The sun god. Appeared in many forms. Often shown with the head of a hawk. Became the most important god. Those gods he merged with would often have *Ra* added to their name (e.g., Ra-Atum and Amun-Ra).

ATUM (later RA-ATUM) "The All." The creator god. One of the many forms of Ra. Father of Shu and Tefnut.

SHU   Father of Nut, the sky goddess. It was his duty to hold her above Geb, the earth, to keep the two apart.

TEFNUT   Sister and wife of Shu. A moon goddess. Mother of Nut and Geb.

NUT   The sky goddess, held in place by her father, Shu. Sister and wife of Geb. Mother of Osiris, Isis, Seth, and Nephthys.

GEB   The earth itself. All plants and trees grew from his back. Brother and husband of Nut. Father of Osiris, Isis, Seth, and Nephthys.

OSIRIS   Ruler of the dead in the Kingdom of the West. Brother and husband of Isis. Father of Horus. Often shown with a mummified body, wrapped in bandages.

ISIS   Goddess of fertility. A mistress of magic. Sister and wife of Osiris. Mother of Horus. Became the most powerful of all the gods and goddesses.

SETH (sometimes SET)   God of chaos and confusion. Evil son of Geb and Nut.

HORUS   Son of Isis and Osiris. Had the head of a falcon and a human body.

ANUBIS   Jackal-headed god of the dead. Assistant to Osiris.

AMUN (later AMUN-RA)   King of the gods in later mythology; later seen as another manifestation of Ra.

BASTET (sometimes BAST)   The mother goddess, often shown as a cat. Daughter of Ra. Sister of Hathor and Sekhmet.

HATHOR   Worshiped as a cow. Sometimes took the form of an angry lioness. Daughter of Ra. Sister of Bastet and Sekhmet.

SEKHMET   Lioness-headed daughter of Ra. Sister of Bastet and Hathor.

NOTE FROM THE AUTHOR
Myths and legends from different cultures are told in very different ways. The purpose of this book is to tell new versions of these old stories, not to try to copy the way in which they might have been traditionally told. They can be read on their own or one after the other, like a story. I hope that you enjoy them and that this book will make you want to find out more about the ancient Egyptians.

THE MURDER OF A GOD

Ra, the mighty sun god, made Osiris and Isis the king and queen of Egypt. Though they were gods, they walked among humans, bringing wisdom and understanding. All would have been well, if their brother, Seth, had not been jealous of their power.

The people of Egypt loved their king and queen. Osiris and Isis made the lives of their subjects good. They taught the Egyptian people the best way to grow and harvest their crops and brought law and order to the land so that everyone was treated fairly. In return the Egyptians learned about the gods and how they should worship them. The people were happy, the gods were happy, and the country of Egypt prospered.

But the time came when Osiris decided that he must spread good fortune among all the countries of the earth, not just Egypt.

"It is only right that other peoples should learn how to make the most of their land and how to bring peace and happiness upon themselves," he said to his wife one day.

"That is true, brother and husband," agreed Isis. "Let us send messengers to foreign parts and spread the news of the power and wisdom of Ra."

Osiris shook his head.

"This is a journey I must make myself," he said. "If the people see that it is a god offering such gifts of inventiveness and prosperity, they will be far more willing to accept them and more willing to change their lives for the better."

"But what of our people–the Egyptians? Who will look over them while you are gone?" frowned Isis.

Osiris put his hand on his wife's shoulder.

"Why, you of course, sister. You are my queen. You are as greatly loved and respected as I am." He smiled. "You must remain here and govern our kingdom in my absence."

"Very well," said Isis. She knew that Osiris was right. It was only fair and just that the gods should share their gifts with all peoples of the earth. And Osiris, the king of Egypt, was the ideal choice to undertake this important task.

Isis felt confident that she could rule Egypt in his absence, as he had suggested. But there was something that bothered her. Some*one*, in fact. That someone was their brother, Seth. Seth had never told Osiris or Isis that he wanted to be ruler of Egypt–that he thought it unfair that his brother had been made king, and not him. But Isis could tell. She knew Seth too well. She could hear the jealousy in his voice when he spoke. She could see the way he tried to control his rage at what he thought was the unfairness of it all.

So after some preparation Osiris left the kingdom of Egypt and began his travel through foreign lands. The journey was a long one, as he visited country after country. Meanwhile, back at the palace, Isis waited for Seth to make his move to try to seize the throne . . . but nothing happened.

Seth spent much of his time in the palace with the courtiers. Whenever he saw Isis, he treated her with the respect befitting her role of queen. He was polite and often friendly, but still Isis did not trust him.

What Isis did not know was that the crafty Seth was making friends with some disgruntled courtiers. However good life may be, there are always greedy people who want more. Egypt was prosperous. Life was good. But these selfish men wanted things to be even more prosperous and even better for *them*.

Seth exploited this weakness. He made these foolish, greedy courtiers his allies.

"When I am king of Egypt, I shall not forget my friends. Those who help me now will be richly rewarded later," Seth whispered to his conspirators in a dark corner, far away from Isis in her throne room. "And I do mean *richly* rewarded."

"But who is to say the people will obey you, if you seize the throne while your brother, the king, is away?" asked one of the courtiers.

"There will be no seizing of the throne," said Seth. "We must bide our time. Let my brother return and be welcomed with open arms."

"And then?"

"Then?" Seth grinned. "Then we shall put my plan into action!"

When King Osiris finally returned, there was much rejoicing in the kingdom. Isis, his queen, was the first to greet him.

"Welcome home, husband and brother," she cried. "I missed you so."

"We all have," said Seth, stepping out from behind his sister's throne. An evil smile flitted across his lips, but only Isis seemed to notice it. And she was not going to let Seth spoil such a joyous occasion.

There was dancing and acrobatics, feasting and song. The festivities went on for several days. Osiris was back at his wife's side and among his own people. And still Seth did not strike. He was waiting . . . waiting for his chance to come.

And come it did, in the form of an invitation for a grand banquet that was to be held at the royal palace. On this particular night Queen Isis would not be present. This was what Seth had been so patiently waiting for. Without his sister's watchful eyes on him, he would be able to put his plan into action.

The banquet was also attended by the small group of disgruntled courtiers who had become Seth's allies. Before Seth arrived, they had begun spreading rumors about a fabulous chest Seth had been given.

"They say that it is made of the finest woods by the greatest craftsmen," said one.

"I hear the gilding is so rich, it gleams like the sun," said another.

"I have been told that it is more beautiful than many of the king's own treasures," whispered another, just loud enough to be sure that his words reached Osiris' ears.

By the time Seth entered the banquet hall–deliberately late so as to make a grand entrance–all talk was of his fabulous golden chest.

"Is it true that you have such a fine treasure?" asked Osiris.

"Yes, brother," said Seth. "I will have it brought to the palace after we have eaten."

So the great feast began. Some time later, just as the banquet was reaching its end, a group of servants brought in the golden chest. A murmur of awe and delight went around the room. This chest was indeed beautiful.

"I have an idea!" said Seth. "Let's see if anyone can fit inside my chest exactly–head touching one end, feet the other. Whoever fits in best can keep the chest as his prize!"

What the guests, including King Osiris, didn't know was that Seth's idea was really part of a carefully laid plan.

As rehearsed, one of the conspirators rushed forward and lay down inside the open chest, while others lined up behind him or encouraged others to join in. Some were too tall for the chest, having to bend their knees to fit. Others were too short.

Finally the only person not to have climbed into the chest was King Osiris himself.

"Brother?" said Seth. "Will you not join the fun?"

Osiris paused for a moment. Then he spoke. "Why not!" he laughed. The king stepped into the trunk and lay down. He was surprised to find that he fitted perfectly. This was no surprise to Seth. He had ordered the craftsmen to build the chest to his exact specifications– so that it would make the perfect *coffin* for his brother.

With the conspirators crowding around the chest so that the other guests couldn't see what was happening, Seth slammed down the lid of the chest, drew the heavy bolts into place, and sealed it shut with molten lead. His cronies then stood back to reveal the smiling Seth standing next to the chest.

"We have no winner," he said. "The chest remains my own."

With that, his greedy allies lifted up the chest and carried it from the room. Inside, the chest was airless and sealed as tight as a tomb. It was such a perfect fit that there was no room for Osiris to bend his legs and kick the lid or to raise his arms and bang the sides. He was trapped. His cries for help were muffled and could not be heard. Then what little air there was ran out, and unable to breathe, the king of Egypt died. Without lifting a finger against Osiris, his brother, Seth, had murdered him.

Under the cover of darkness, the makeshift coffin was carried to the banks of the Nile and thrown into the river. The next morning Seth announced the tragic death of his brother and proclaimed himself king. He was crowned that day.

When news of her husband's death reached Queen Isis, she broke down and wept. She then dressed in widow's clothes and cut off a lock of her hair. But the time for full grieving would have to wait. She knew that she must find out how King Osiris had died and what had happened to his body.

THE SEARCH FOR OSIRIS

Turned away from her own palace by the order of the new king, her evil brother Seth, Isis went from village to village trying to learn the truth about what had happened to her murdered husband. There were many different rumors, but she finally learned the truth from a group of children.

The children told the former queen of Egypt that they had seen some men throw a chest into the Nile. It was a beautiful chest–they could see that in the torchlight–and they had heard the men boasting to one another that the body of the dead king, Osiris, was inside. When the men had gone, the children had come out of the shadows and watched the chest being carried downriver by the current.

"Then there is hope still!" said Isis, a feeling of joy welling up inside her. She hurried along the riverbank, following the flow of the river and hoping beyond hope that the chest had washed up on the bank. She journeyed on until she reached the sea, yet there was no sign of the chest. But still she would not give in.

Isis made her way northward along the coastline and heard reports of sightings of a strange and beautiful chest floating in the sea. She never saw it with her own eyes, but she felt sure that she would catch up with it soon.

The goddess passed through country after country, following reports of the chest, until she reached the kingdom of Byblos.

There the talk was not of a golden chest in the sea but of a fabulous tamarisk tree that had sprung up overnight on the shore.

Isis found out that King Melcarthus of Byblos had had the tamarisk tree cut down and brought back to the city to be turned into a pillar for his palace. She was convinced that the magical tree must have something to do with Osiris' coffin, and she hurried to the palace.

When the goddess arrived, she sat in a courtyard close to the entrance and waited. Of course, she could have used her power to steal the pillar and discover its secret. But she did not want to. There had been enough abuse of power from her brother Seth. She would bide her time and find another way into the palace.

She didn't have to wait long. A number of maids to Queen Athenais of Byblos left the palace and caught sight of Isis. It was obvious from her beauty and appearance that she wasn't from those parts, so they hurried over to ask her where she was from. Their mistress loved gossip from afar, and this mysterious woman might have news to pass on.

Isis explained that she had come all the way from Egypt. Then she offered to plait one of the maid's hair in the latest fashion. Her hands were so quick and so skilled that the girl was delighted with the result, and soon Isis had plaited the hair of each and every maid.

"Did you add oils?" asked one. "What is that beautiful smell?"

What they didn't realize was that as she plaited, Isis breathed upon each girl and–because she was a goddess and a mistress of magic–the divine smell of her breath clung to their skin.

When it was time to go back to the palace, the young maids were reluctant to leave.

"Thank you!" they smiled, as they hurried through the entrance.

Queen Athenais was instantly charmed by her maids' new hairstyles, but it was the fragrance that delighted her most.

"It must be one of those fine new Egyptian perfumes we hear so much about," she said. "Send for this woman at once!"

So Isis, in the guise of an ordinary woman, was brought before the queen, who asked that she plait and perfume her hair. This Isis did, and Athenais was very pleased. She asked Isis to stay.

That night Isis crept into the room where the new pillar stood. It was made from the single trunk of the incredible tree that had sprung up on the shore. Placing her hand against the smooth wood, she instantly understood what had happened. Her husband's coffin had washed ashore and become entwined with the roots of a young tamarisk tree. Though dead, some of Osiris' godly powers had somehow seeped from the sealed chest, causing the sapling to grow into an enormous tree, with the god in his coffin in the middle. . . . Osiris' body was inside this very pillar! Weeping, Isis returned to bed.

In a short space of time, Queen Athenais of Byblos became very fond of Isis, and Isis became fond of her and her baby son, whom she now looked after. Isis was content to stay at the palace, near the body of her beloved dead husband. By day she acted as a devoted nanny to the prince. By night she was a widow grieving for her husband inside his pillar coffin.

As time went on, Isis came to love the prince so much that she could not bear to think of him dying, as Osiris had done. Each night she took the sleeping boy with her into the room with the pillar. She started a magical fire that burned brightly with the flames of mortality. Carefully she placed the prince at the very heart of it, and each night a little more of his mortality burned away. Eventually he would be able to live forever.

While she waited for this process to be complete, Isis turned herself into a bird and flew around and around the pillar that housed Osiris' body inside the golden chest.

Intrigued and worried by reports of the newcomer's secret visits to the hall, Queen Athenais burst into the room one night. She screamed at the terrible sight of her youngest son apparently on fire.

She snatched him from the flames and held him close to her, just as Isis turned from a swallow back into human form.

"Sorceress!" cried the queen. "Stay away from me!"

Understanding the woman's fear, the goddess was quick to calm her. She explained that the flames could not have harmed her son, but now that he had been snatched from the magic fire, he could not live forever. She then explained who she really was and why she was there.

Relieved that the prince was not harmed, but saddened that she had interrupted a spell that would have allowed him to live forever, Athenais asked how she could serve the goddess Isis.

Isis asked for permission to remove the pillar, and Athenais readily agreed. The goddess cut away the trunk and removed the chest within.

King Melcarthus and Queen Athenais then gave the goddess the finest ship in their fleet and a crew to sail it for her. The next morning Isis bade them farewell and began her return journey with Osiris in the chest.

Back on land once again, Isis ordered the crew to carry the chest into the desert, away from prying eyes. Then she had it carried to the swamps of Buto, in case news of its discovery reached Seth. From time to time she opened the coffin and looked at Osiris' body. He looked so peaceful, almost as if he were asleep and not dead.

While Isis herself was sleeping one night, Seth appeared in the swamp. His spies were everywhere, and he had learned of where the chest had been hidden.

Lifting the lid, he looked down at the body of the brother he had murdered.

"You look so perfect," he sneered. "You look so whole. What if our dear sister's magic is strong enough to breathe life back into you? You could simply climb out. . . . I must make sure that can never happen."

With that he heaved the body from the coffin and cut it into 14 pieces. He then scattered the pieces all over Egypt.

"Let my sister try to make you whole again now!" he said, a sneer forming on his cruel lips.

When Isis found the body of her husband gone and learned what had happened to it, she cried out in anguish and despair.

Her wailing was so loud and so painful that it reached the ears of Isis' sister, Nephthys, who was Seth's own wife. Nephthys felt so sorry for Isis that she decided to help her to gather together the pieces of their murdered brother's body.

This dreadful task was a long one and took many years, but at long last all the pieces were reunited. Some say that Anubis, the god with the head of a jackal, helped the sisters. Then, using her greatest magic, Isis made Osiris' body whole again.

Yet Isis was not able to give the body life. Instead, Ra, the sun god, made Osiris' spirit Ruler of the Dead in the Kingdom of the West. From then on when people died, their spirits were judged and were given the chance of an afterlife.

THE FIGHT FOR THE THRONE

Despite Osiris' death Ra made it possible for Isis to have the king's son. His name was Horus, and when he grew up, he claimed the right to rule Egypt as his father's heir.

Seth was furious. He'd murdered his brother, Osiris, so that he could claim the throne, and now Osiris' son wanted it from him. . . . Well, he certainly wasn't going to give up without a fight. If the need arose, perhaps he would slaughter this troublemaker, too. He had tried to kill Horus as a baby and failed, but he would not fail a second time. In the meantime he would go about trying to solve this dispute in a different way.

The matter was brought before a tribunal of the gods. Each and every one sided with Horus.

"His claim is true," said Shu, who, as the eldest son of Ra, took it upon himself to head the proceedings.

"Justice is on his side," agreed another.

"Seth seized the throne by force," said another. "It is Horus' birthright."

"So we are all agreed then," said Shu. The other gods and goddesses nodded their agreement. "Then let it be known that, by a unanimous decision—"

"Unanimous?" demanded Seth. "Does that mean each and every one present is against me?"

Shu looked around at the assembled gods and goddesses.

"Yes," he said.

"But am I not a god?" said Seth, a cruel smile playing across his lips.

"Indeed. One who uses force and treachery—"

Seth interrupted once more. "So, I am a god, and I say that the throne is mine . . . which means that this is not a unanimous decision."

"You cannot have a voice," said Shu. "You are one of those being judged. It has been decided—"

"How dare you decide," boomed a voice. And it was not Seth who interrupted this time, but Ra himself. "Why has not one of you consulted me on this matter? Am I not the creator? Am I not Khepri in the morning, Ra at noon, and Atum in the evening? Am I not the molder of mountains? Am I not lord of all the gods?"

"Y-Yes," said Shu, somewhat shaken.

"Yet you do not think to consult me on this matter?" demanded Ra.

"But Horus is so obviously in the right!" Isis protested.

"As if my sister—his own *mother*—would be unbiased!" Seth complained. "She has always been against me!"

"Seth speaks the truth," said Ra, still angered that he had been left out of the proceedings. It must have been obvious to him that Seth's claim was weak, but he seemed to take his side to annoy the others. "We will decide this another way!"

"How?" sighed Isis, with a sinking heart. Her son had been about to take up his rightful place. Now it had all gone wrong. "How can anyone give the throne of Egypt to the uncle while the son and heir still lives?" she demanded.

"How can the throne be taken from an elder and given to a mere youngster?" returned Ra.

The arguments raged on, with many a different judge chosen then rejected by one side or the other. In the end it was Horus and Seth who agreed how the matter would be decided. They would face each other in a series of challenges, and the victor would become ruler of Egypt.

During one terrible fight, Seth and Horus turned into hippopotamuses and fought each other in the Nile. Their huge jaws locked together. Isis, watching from the bank, was so worried that they would both drown that she fired a harpoon at Seth.

Unfortunately for Horus, his mother's aim was not accurate. The point pierced Horus' leg. This gave Seth the advantage. If Isis hadn't fired again and hit Seth this time, it could have been the end of Horus.

Seth writhed in agony, the harpoon embedded deep in his flesh.

"How can you do this to me, Isis?" he cried. "I am your brother!"

"My father was your brother," Horus bellowed. "And remember what you did to him!"

But Isis took pity on Seth and used her magic to remove the harpoon. The first contest was over, without a clear winner.

Another time Seth found Horus sleeping by an oasis and ripped out an eye–some say both–but, thanks to Hathor, Horus' wife, it was restored to him and his sight made well again.

And so the fights continued. Sometimes Horus used cunning instead of strength. On one such occasion he insisted that they have a boat race. But this was to be no ordinary boat race.

"The boats must be made of stone," said Horus.

"But that's impossible!" Seth protested. "Stone boats will sink!"

"If I can make a boat of stone, then surely the great Seth can?" said Horus cunningly.

"Very well," said Seth, rising to the challenge, "but you must promise me that you will not use any of your mother's magic to assist you. This fight is between us."

"You have my word!" Horus fumed, embarrassed by the suggestion that he should think of asking Isis for help.

So Seth went away and built himself a boat of stone. When he came to the water's edge, Horus' boat was already in the river. It appeared to have been carved from one solid piece of rock but was floating on the surface. It looked no heavier than a log.

Seth was impressed and pushed his own boat into the Nile. It sank to the riverbed with him inside it.

"I win!" said Horus, trying to hide his laughter.

With a roar of pure rage, Seth turned himself into a hippopotamus once more and launched himself at Horus. When his massive jaws closed around the boat, he found that it was not made of stone at all– it was a wooden boat covered with a rough plaster to look like stone.

The gods who were watching saw it, too.

"Stop this!" Ra ordered, and Seth had to obey. This latest challenge was declared void, just like all the others. Both had cheated: Horus with his boat, and Seth by changing into a hippopotamus.

Isis used her magic in many ways to try to help her son, Horus, win the throne, which she knew was his by right. Once she changed herself into a beautiful woman, dressed as a widow in mourning. She sat in a place where she knew Seth would be walking. When Seth came upon her, she was crying.

"Why are you so sad?" he asked, dazzled by her beauty.

"My husband is dead and our cattle have been taken," she wailed.

"Tell me what happened," said Seth, putting his arm around her. She really was the most beautiful woman he had ever seen.

"My husband was a herdsman, and when he died, the cattle and our home became the property of my son," sobbed Isis, in disguise. "But now a stranger has come and taken everything from us. He claims it as his."

Seth looked at the widow. He found it hard to imagine that a lowly herdsman could have been married to such a beautiful woman. Such a woman was worthy of being married to a *god*. How could this stranger do such a thing?

"How dare a stranger seize your husband's property while his son is still alive!" he roared.

Isis laughed and changed shape again–this time into a bird that flew up into a tree and squawked in delight at the trap her brother had walked into.

"So someone shouldn't steal a man's property while his son still lives!" she cried. "Does that include the throne of Egypt? You've condemned yourself out of your own mouth, brother. The throne belongs to Horus, and you know it."

Isis informed the other gods of Seth's admission, but still he would not give in.

Some say that it was Osiris himself, now Ruler of the Dead, who finally forced the gods to decide in favor of his son and place him on the throne. There were demons in his kingdom who owed no loyalty to any god but him—not even Ra—and Osiris threatened to release them onto the earth if the matter was not settled.

Other versions tell how it was one named Neith who made the final decision. Neith was Ra's mother, which made her mother of the creator himself. She ruled that Horus must become king. If not, she would bring the heavens crashing down and end the world.

After 80 years of fighting, Horus and Seth were at peace. Horus ruled a contented Egypt for many years and was the forefather of all the pharaohs that followed.

THE END OF HUMANKIND

For a time Ra dwelt on the earth in one of his many forms, so that he could live among his people. He was greatly revered and respected until finally he began to grow old.

In appearance Ra was obviously not the great and powerful god he had once been. Was this really the lord of all gods, the god of light and health? He certainly didn't look too healthy. He had bones like silver, skin like gold, and hair the color of lapis lazuli–a deep blue that reminded people of the graying hair of an old man.

Soon people's respect was gone, and in time that lack of respect turned to open mockery.

"Why should we look up to him?" they muttered. "Soon he will be gone. Why do we need to honor him anyway?"

Ra was furious when he heard that this was the way his own creations treated him. Myth has it that the first humans were born from his own tears, yet now people treated him as if he were no more important in their lives than a speck of dirt.

Many humans openly conspired to be rid of him.

"Let us destroy this old god so that we can rule our own destiny," they said. Like rebellious children turning against a compassionate father, they became the worst kind of traitors.

Ra summoned the god Nu, for it was out of the ancient waters of Nu that Ra himself had first risen.

"Many of the humans I created now despise me," he told Nu.

"I intend to destroy them, but seek your counsel first. Is such a punishment right?"

"The humans were born from your tears," said Nu, "and do you not call your daughter Hathor your 'eye'? Does she not see for you and report back what she sees?"

"Yes," said Ra. "Go on."

"Then would it not be fitting for your eye to wipe away your tears . . . to destroy them for you?" suggested Nu.

"Yes!" said Ra, his anger bursting to the surface. "I will send Hathor to kill the ungrateful people I created–all of them, down to the last man, woman, and child!"

Ra sent instructions that Shu, Tefnut, Geb, and Nut must come to his palace in secret. He also sent a special message to his daughter Hathor, informing her that he had an important mission for her.

Soon everyone arrived at the palace, but it was hard to keep such a gathering of gods and goddesses a secret. News leaked out to the people that Ra was assembling his forces around him.

Those men and women who had spoken openly against him began to feel afraid. Some left their homes and families and went to hide out in the deserts of the Red Land.

"I intend to destroy those who have turned against me," Ra announced to the gods and goddesses. "Their time on this earth is at an end."

"All of humankind, or only those who have betrayed you?" asked one god.

"Each and every one!" Nu cried. "Soon they will all turn against Ra, so let us put an end to them."

"Yes!" said Ra, whipped into a frenzy of hatred. How dare people speak of him as if he were a dithering old fool! He was the creator. He gave them life . . . and he could just as easily take it away. "That duty lies with you, daughter," he told Hathor. "You have many forms. Most know you for your kindly nature as a moon goddess or for your cow's head with gentle eyes, but I want you to take on your wildest form–become a lioness and tear them limb from limb."

Ra's punishment was swift and terrible. His daughter Hathor, now a terrifying and ferocious lioness, began by tracking down the traitors.

After a full day of killing, she returned to her father at his palace. She was exhausted, and her fur was matted with the blood of her victims. He welcomed her and told her to rest.

Inside, Ra was tormented. Now that the killing had begun, he'd had a change of heart. Perhaps it was fair enough to destroy the betrayers, but all day he had been plagued with the dying cries of the innocent. The prayers of his loyal followers had filled his head, yet still he had let his daughter kill them in her terrifying blood lust —a blood lust that had been brought about by his own orders. Death was no solution. He hadn't created the human race just so that he could destroy it.

But Ra could not go back on his word. At a time when people—and possibly some of the gods and goddesses—were beginning to doubt his strength and absolute power, he could not afford to show such open weakness or indecision. He had given Hathor her instructions, and he could not go back on them. He would have to come up with a way of saving what was left of the human race while Hathor slept.

Ra knew that he could waste no time. That night he called his personal messengers to him.

"Run faster than shadows to Aswan and bring me back ocher," he commanded, and specified a very large amount. (Ocher is a kind of earth that is very red. It was often used in paints and dyes.)

While the messengers were on their mission, sworn to secrecy, and Hathor slept—still in the form of a dreadful lioness and dreaming of her killings—Ra sent for his High Priest at the city of Heliopolis. The High Priest threw himself at the feet of the god.

"How can I serve you mighty Ra?" he asked. He had seen the killing and knew that the creator was angry with his creations.

Ra pointed to a stack of baskets, brought to him by his messengers.

"Take these and have the ocher within them mixed in 7,000 jars of barley beer. This most important of tasks must be completed before daybreak."

"It will be done," said the High Priest, and he hurried away. With the help of an army of slave girls, the red soil was soon mixed in the jars of barley beer, turning the liquid thick and red.

Next Ra led the High Priest and a long line of slave girls into the night. The 7,000 jars were carried between them. Everyone was forbidden to speak or make a sound. This noiseless army, unknowingly on a mission to save humankind itself, snaked silently through the night. Finally they reached the place that Ra had chosen.

At daybreak, on a silent signal from their god and master, the slave girls poured the contents of each jar onto the earth, and soon there was a huge pool of sticky red liquid before them.

"Your work is done," said Ra, turning to leave. "Tell no one."

Later that morning Hathor woke refreshed. Still in the form of a terrifying lioness, she was prepared to carry out her father's orders and to kill more humans. This would teach them not to speak of Ra with disrespect . . . not that this would be a lesson people could pass on to their children. Soon all humans would be dead!

The smell of human blood was already in her nostrils, and she was ready to begin. Running at the speed of a lioness on a hunt, Hathor reached the place where she had left off the day before.

In front of her was an huge pool of what looked like human blood.

Delighted, she began to lap at it as a cat laps milk. It tasted good. She drank more and more. What she didn't know was that this was not blood, but bright red barley beer . . . and, goddess or not, drinking so much beer made her drunk and drowsy.

Soon Hathor abandoned her mission to destroy the human race. She had no wish to kill and no lust for blood. All she wanted to do . . . was . . . sleep. . . . Walking unsteadily on her four massive paws, Hathor staggered back to the palace with a smile on her leonine face.

"Greetings, daughter," said Ra, and Hathor laid her head on his lap. She forgot all thoughts of killing and fell into a deep, deep sleep. Stroking her fur, Ra was content. Honor had been satisfied and humankind saved.

Sometimes when the Nile floods, the water washes over ocher and turns red. Perhaps this was where Ra got the idea. Or perhaps Ra made this happen as a reminder that he could so easily have destroyed all humankind.

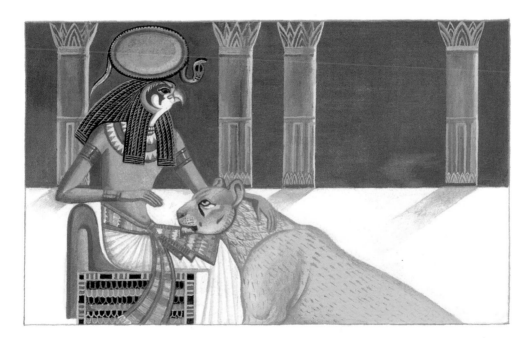

The Pharaoh and the Thief

This gripping story tells of a locked room filled with treasure, a headless corpse, and a cunning villain. Though no pharaoh called Rhampsinitus actually existed, some experts believe that this story could have grown up from real events.

Rhampsinitus was fabulously rich, even by a pharaoh's standard, and his greatest fear was that his treasures would be stolen. Even pyramids—the tombs of his ancestors—were not safe from robbers, despite their traps and secret passages. Rhampsinitus therefore decided that he would have a special stone building constructed to house his riches. He summoned the finest architect, instructed him to design such a house, and studied the plans in the minutest detail before permitting the work to begin.

Only the most trustworthy were put to work on the project, and all workers were overseen by the architect himself. When the building was completed, Rhampsinitus gave it a final inspection. It was one single room. The walls, ceiling, and floor were built of solid stone. There were no windows, and there was only one door. Satisfied, Rhampsinitus had the building filled with his treasures and positioned his guards in front of the door. He then stamped his seal onto the entrance so that no one could enter without breaking it and revealing their crime.

Time went by, and though other robberies were carried out through the kingdom, the pharaoh's treasures remained safe.

It was only after the architect who had built this giant stone strongbox died that strange things began to happen.

On one occasion, when Rhampsinitus swept past his guards, broke the seal on the door, and went into the room to admire his treasure trove, he felt that something was different. He couldn't tell if anything was missing. He had so much treasure—statuettes, amulets, perfume, golden furniture, and silver—in piles all around the room that it would be impossible to remember where everything was. But something didn't feel quite right.

The guards were insistent that no one had got past them, and they reminded the pharaoh that the seal had been unbroken until he himself had entered. Puzzled, Rhampsinitus put a fresh seal on the door and attended to the matters of the day.

A week later, when the pharaoh next entered his strong room, he was in no doubt that items were missing this time. There were gaps. He had been robbed! As puzzled as he was enraged, Rhampsinitus placed traps among the treasure, resealed the room, and doubled the number of guards at the door. Now he would catch this clever thief!

The next morning the pharaoh was greeted with a sight he'd most certainly not expected. A man had, indeed, been caught in one of the traps. Its metal jaws had the villain by the leg, so he wasn't able to flee . . . but that wasn't the only reason why this man was going nowhere. The captured thief had no head.

"How can this be possible?" raged the pharaoh. "No one can have tunneled through the floor. It is solid rock, as are the walls and ceiling. The door remained sealed and guarded . . . yet this man's head is missing along with my treasure!"

He ordered the body to be hung from the palace walls, as a warning to any other robbers who might try to steal his treasure. This was a terrible thing to do, for even a thief had the right to be given a proper funeral. It was for the gods to judge the dead man.

"Look out for those who cry at the sight of the body," Rhampsinitus instructed. "They might be the thief's accomplices or members of his family and must be brought to me. I *will* solve this mystery!"

So the body was hung up for all to see, and although many were horrified by the cruelty of it, no one cried. Then the body was stolen.

The theft was boldly executed with great cunning. It began when a man apparently came to deliver wine to the palace. Instead of the usual jars, the wine was in goats' skins strapped to the backs of his donkeys. As the animals were led past the guards at the palace entrance, a few skins fell to the ground, the stoppers came out, and wine spilled onto the ground. The guards hurried forward to snatch them up, and the man thanked them for saving what precious wine they could. He gave them a half-spilled, half-full skin to thank them, and they insisted that he drink it with them.

Soon the guards had drunk far too much and, after much laughing and joking, fell asleep. It was while they were in this drunken stupor that the so-called wine merchant cut down the headless body, put it on the back of one of his donkeys, and rode away into the night.

When Pharaoh Rhampsinitus was informed of what had happened, he was furious. The guards had woken with splitting headaches from having drunk too much wine . . . but this pain was nothing compared to the punishment they received for their carelessness. Despite everything Rhampsinitus couldn't help but have a sneaking admiration for this clever thief who always seemed to be one step ahead of him.

Now it was the pharaoh's turn to be cunning. He guessed that the one thing any clever villain probably liked to do almost as much as stealing was to brag about it. What was the point of committing daring crimes if you couldn't tell anyone?

So Rhampsinitus announced that he would give his daughter's hand to the man who revealed the cleverest secret, no matter how wicked. All they had to do was visit the princess and tell her in confidence.

Once she had heard the confessions, she would choose the winner.

Of course, there was only one confession the pharaoh was really interested in, and that was the thief's. It was agreed that if the thief came, the princess would clasp his hand and then call for the guards, who would spring into action.

Sure enough, the thief came. He was looking nervously from side to side and had a cloak wrapped around him in great folds. The story he had to tell was a remarkable one.

"My father was your father's chief architect," he explained. "He built the stone room where your father keeps his treasure. He designed it and watched over its construction, but no one was watching over *him*. One of the stones was in fact two, so perfectly interlocking that no one could see the join. My father told this secret to my brother and me just before he died. We found the stones, slid them apart, and crawled through the gap."

The princess listened in wonder.

"The first few times my brother and I entered the room, we only took a few things, so that they wouldn't be missed. As time went on, we became greedier, until your father laid the traps," continued the thief, a sad look crossing his face. "My brother was caught in one, and his leg was badly broken. He was in great pain, and there was no way of escape. He insisted that I cut off his head. He'd rather have a quick death than die in agony . . . and if I took my poor brother's head with me, no one could identify him and come after me or my family."

Rhampsinitus' daughter was spellbound by the thief's confession.

"I returned the head to my mother, and we buried it," said the thief. "Later I reclaimed his body. It has been reunited with the head, and my brother has received a proper burial. Now, sad though it is, isn't that the best confession you have heard?"

"Oh, yes," smiled the princess, admiring his cleverness, but also happy at the thought of how pleased her father would be to capture this man. "Give me your hand."

"Very well," said the man. An arm appeared out of the folds of the cloak, and the princess clutched the hand, which was strangely cold.

So this is how the rough hand of a thief feels, she thought. Gripping it tightly, she called out for the guards.

By the time they had piled into the room, the cunning thief was nowhere to be seen. And the princess was screaming. She was holding a human hand, but there was nothing at the other end of the arm! It hadn't been his own arm that he put forward from under the folds of his coat. It was one he must have stolen from an embalming shop before going to the palace. He was cunning enough to have known from the outset that this was a trap, but he wouldn't have missed telling his story for anything!

Rhampsinitus was so impressed and amazed by this latest turn of events that he announced a rich reward and a free pardon to the thief, if he gave himself up. The thief believed him, and the pharaoh was true to his word.

As it turned out, the clever thief received far greater rewards. He was not only given the princess's hand in marriage but was also made a minister. And why not? He was one of the cleverest men in Egypt!

SHIPWRECKED ON THE ISLAND OF KA

This legend includes a tale within a tale within a tale. It begins with a ship sailing back to Egypt from a mission in Nubia. The mission is led by an envoy, under orders to bring back riches for the pharaoh. The mission has failed, and the envoy knows that the pharaoh does not take kindly to failure.

The envoy was standing alone in the bow of the ship, staring up at the stars, when one of his fellow sailors came to stand beside him.

"What is wrong, sire?" the sailor asked.

The envoy looked at the sailor, who was, like him, a well-respected official to the pharaoh's royal court.

"This whole mission has been a disaster," he sighed. "Tomorrow I must face the pharaoh with little to show for our journey."

"A disaster?" said the sailor. "You cannot call it that. No one has been lost at sea or died on land. Surely that counts for something?"

"I do not think the pharaoh will see it that way," the envoy said, with a heavy heart.

The sailor smiled.

"Things don't always turn out the way one might expect," he said. "Take me, for example. You know me as a successful courtier, but it was not always that way. I was a poor sailor once, and not only that, I was on an expedition that truly was disastrous." And so he began to tell the envoy his amazing tale.

"It was my first voyage, and I was bursting with pride to be one of such a fine crew," said the sailor. "There were 120 of us, each handpicked. The ship was huge and my fellow sailors fearless. They knew everything there was to know about sailing. If a sailor can ever feel safe when out at sea, it is among such men.

"How foolish I was to forget that we are all in the hands of the gods. Our ship was crossing the Red Sea, bound for the royal turquoise mines, when disaster struck. A dreadful storm came up out of nowhere, and every one of us was ill-prepared. There was a cruel wind, crashing waves, and driving rain. Our ship was battered and beaten in every direction until one huge wave–unimaginable in its force and size– washed over us and drowned every single living thing on board, except for me.

"That same wave that killed my fellow crewmen picked me up and dashed me onto the shore of some unknown island. Cold, soaked through, and in a daze, I summoned all my strength to drag myself onto the beach, out of the water. With one final effort I pulled myself under a pile of driftwood to shelter. There I lay for three whole days and nights."

"Eventually I awoke and managed to drag myself farther inland to try to find food and fresh water to stay alive. I found that the island was a paradise. It was like the most beautiful lush green garden you can imagine. It was filled with trees and grasses and the most luscious fruits and vegetables. There were birds and animals and pools of the coldest water, filled with fish. I cooked myself a feast and then burned an offering to the gods, to thank them for saving my life and for bringing me to such a place of plenty.

"Soon after that the earth beneath me began to shudder, and a strange noise filled my ears. An enormous snake, attracted by the smoke, appeared between the trees. It was of a terrifying beauty, as long as a dozen men, and with scales of gold and lapis lazuli.

It also had a beard like a god's, as long as I am tall! The snake reared up before me as if it were about to strike, then spoke–yes, *spoke*–wanting to know how I came to be on its island.

"I confess that I was too frightened to reply. I threw myself at its mercy. What else could I do? Before I fully knew what was happening, the snake had picked me up in its jaws. I felt sure that it was going to eat me, but I was too paralyzed with terror to utter a plea for mercy or a cry for help. But instead of harming me, it took me to its lair.

"There it put me down and questioned me a second time.

" 'How did you come to be here, little one?' There was a trace of kindness in the giant snake's voice, and this time I plucked up enough courage to reply. I told it of the voyage to the mines, of the terrible storm, and of the 119 men who had drowned.

"Then I made an amazing discovery. This huge creature was gentle and kind. He–for I came to think of him as 'he' and not 'it'–urged me not to be afraid, but to rejoice that I was saved.

" 'You were right to offer thanks to the gods,' he said. 'They have chosen to save you from the waters so that you may live here with me for four months. After that time you will be rescued by a crew of a passing ship. They will take you back to Egypt, and it is there that you will die as an old man.'

"Of course, I was amazed by this and also relieved, for as you well know, to die away from Egypt and one's family means that the proper preparations and ceremonies cannot take place, and the spirit may not reach the Kingdom of the West. But I was still saddened at the death of all my fellow sailors.

"The giant snake could understand those feelings, too. He bent his head close to mine, his forked tongue flicking in and out as he spoke.

" 'I know what it is to lose those close to you, little one,' he said sadly. 'I am all alone on this island now, but it was not always so. My whole family used to share this paradise with me–my brothers, sisters, wife, and children. There were 75 of us in all, and our lives were ones of sharing and happiness. But one day it all ended. A shooting star fell from the heavens and killed every one of them.

For a long time after that, I wished that I, too, had been engulfed in the flames. Without them I felt so hopeless and alone. I share your pain.'

"I was deeply moved by the story this magnificent creature had told me. All trace of fear I had felt was now gone.

" 'When I return to Egypt, as you have foretold, I will inform the pharaoh of your magnificence and kindness,' I told him. 'I will ask him to send you gifts of fragrant oils and exotic treasures.'

"But the snake laughed. He knew that I was a poor sailor, not a wealthy man, and that I would not have the attention of the pharaoh.

" 'And what should I want with such gifts?" he then asked. 'I am the Prince of Punt, and this island has more riches than your pharaoh could ever hope to give me. What I will enjoy is your company.' "

"For months we were excellent companions. He called his island the Island of Ka and 'Ka,' as you are aware, is the spirit we all have living within us. I do not think he meant that it was an island of spirits, though. I saw no phantoms there, just beauty. I think it was more of an enchanted place. . . . Then, just as he had predicted, after four months had passed, I saw a ship on the horizon. I think the snake used his powers to bring it closer to the shore, where I hailed it and recognized the crew.

"Happy though I was to be heading home to family and friends, I felt a real sadness at leaving behind the snake with scales of gold and lapis lazuli.

" 'Goodbye, little one,' he said. 'Think kindly of me.'

"I cannot deny that there was a lump in my throat as I accepted the gifts he gave me. There were all kinds of treasures, from rare spices and jewelry to oils and animals. I kissed the ground in front of him and promised him that I would return one day.

" 'You will never find this place again,' he told me. 'Once you are gone, it will be covered by the waves.' He then made another prediction: that I would be home, safe and sound, within two months.

We said our goodbyes, and I took my gifts to the waiting ship.

"When I reached Egypt, I went with the crew to the pharaoh's palace. There I presented him with the gifts that the noble snake had given me. I also told the pharaoh of my extraordinary adventure on the Island of Ka. He was pleased and rewarded me, which is how I come to have the official job I hold today. The snake had said that I would prosper, and he was right."

"So you see," said the sailor to the envoy, in the bow of the ship heading homeward, "a journey that began as a terrible disaster turned out very differently for me. One never can tell."

The envoy studied the sailor's face. Should he believe this man's tale? Why not? He had heard stranger stories. And maybe things wouldn't turn out so badly when he himself faced the pharaoh the very next day.

THE SECRET NAME OF RA

**Isis was the goddess of fertility and of life.
She was a mistress of magic and the wife of
Osiris, Lord of the Underworld. She was cleverer
than countless other gods and goddesses, but she
wanted the greatest power of all–Ra's power.**

The sun god, Ra, had many different forms, and for each form
he had a different name. These names were used in praise
and in prayer throughout Egypt. They were called out to honor
him and to celebrate his importance and his power, except for
one name, that is. For that name was a secret, known only to
the god himself. It was given to him at the beginning of time–
for it was he who had created time–and was hidden deep
within him.

The secret name of Ra was the key to his power. To know
the secret name was to have control over the most powerful of
all the gods. Isis wanted that name.

Few were safe against Isis' magic, but such magic was useless
against Ra, the creator, the greatest god of all. So if she could
not use her magic, how could Isis get the name from him?
Through trickery?

Though all-powerful, Ra did not seem to be the magnificent
god he had been in the beginning. His body had grown old and
frail, and although he was still the greatest force on earth, his
skin had sagged, and sometimes he dribbled out of the side of
his mouth.

An idea began to form in Isis' mind. The way to trick Ra into revealing his secret name would be to harness the sun god's own power and turn it against him!

One morning she joined Ra as he strolled across the earth, surrounded by a group of other gods and goddesses. There were Shu, Tefnut, Seth, Sekhmet, Hathor, Anubis, Toth, and Nephthys, among many others.

Ra's sight was not what it used to be, and he was no longer sure-footed on the soil. Once when he stopped to talk, a drop of his saliva dribbled from his mouth onto the ground. Now was Isis' chance. One drop of the creator's own saliva would be more powerful as a weapon against him than an army of a thousand men!

When the others moved on, Isis stayed behind and carefully scooped up the soil mixed with the creator's drool. Then she slipped away, unnoticed, to her palace. Safe from prying eyes, she kneaded the damp soil until it became a soft clay, and as she labored, she uttered magic words.

All night she worked, whispering her spells so that they mingled with the power of Ra's saliva and with the soil. From this clay she formed a snake. But this was no model. This magical snake was *alive*. Now all Isis had to do was to be patient.

The next morning Ra took his usual path across the earth with the other gods and goddesses. What he didn't know was that Isis had been there before him and had freed the snake in readiness.

Suddenly Ra felt a sharp pain in his ankle. He let out a cry. What could it be? Nothing he had created could hurt him, and he was the creator of all things. Yet the pain was terrible and was spreading up his leg. And with the sharp pain came an inner, twisting agony.

"I am poisoned!" he cried, stumbling to the ground.

The gods and goddesses who accompanied him were stunned. To see the mighty Ra stumble and fall was unthinkable. For him to be poisoned was impossible.

"How can this be happening?" gasped one of the gods attending him.

Ma'at, the winged goddess of justice, dashed forward and caught sight of the snake slithering off into the tall grass. She could not believe her eyes. No snake could poison the lord of the gods.

"Help me!" rasped Ra. "I am dying. I am on fire!"

In turn each god and goddess tried to help him, but their charms and powers were useless against this unknown force that was, moment by moment, taking his life away.

Isis was known to be more clever than a thousand men, and her magic was second only to Ra's. She was the obvious choice to do all she could to save the sun god and was ushered to his aid. He looked even more frail and vulnerable than before as he lay there, his head resting in her lap. Little did anyone know that it was she who had turned Ra's own power against him.

"What happened?" she wailed, pretending to be shocked and to know nothing of events. "How can the Lord of Creation be so ill?"

"Ill? I am dying. I was bitten by a serpent," said the sun god through gritted teeth, as he tried to fight the pain. "But this was no serpent of my making. There is wrongdoing at work here."

"You cannot die, Divine Father," said the goddess.

"I feel it . . . ," said Ra, writhing as the pain burned deeper. Sweat poured from his brow.

"I can save you," said Isis, "but I need to know your name."

"I am Ra. I am Creator of the Heavens and the Earth. I am Khepri in the morning–the scarab beetle, sailing through the sky in the *Boat of Millions of Years*–Ra, the blazing sun at noon, and Atum, the setting sun, in the evening. . . .' He paused and winced with pain. "I am molder of the mountains–"

"These are not the names I mean, lord," said Isis. "These names are known to us all. If I am to save you, I must know your secret name."

"I can tell no one," groaned Ra, "for therein lies my power!"

"You cannot ask that of him," protested another god.

"Without such knowledge I cannot save you, lord," said Isis. "And I cannot let you die. You must tell me."

"How can such a secret help me?" demanded Ra, fighting the pain.

"Because to have someone call out to you in that name is the only cure," Isis explained. "No poison can harm you if you are addressed in the name of ultimate power."

The poison—from a snake created from his own saliva and fueled with his own power—now coursed through Ra's veins. His head began to swim, and everything in front of his eyes became a blur. His mouth was dry and his voice croaked.

"I must tell you," he agreed at last. Mustering his strength, he managed to sit up and issue an order. "Leave us!" he said to the anxious group of gods and goddesses, and though his voice was weak, no one dared to question him. Ra and Isis were left alone together.

"My secret name is my power . . .," said Ra, slowly. "It is buried deep within me. It is a physical thing . . . and I give it to you alone."

Reader, I cannot tell you what that name was. But I can tell you that Ra passed it on to Isis, and she felt her body filling with a new power.

In Egypt there are monuments called obelisks, pointing upward to the sky. Each is built to the glory of Ra and is covered in the sacred writing of hieroglyphs, praising the sun god and listing his many names. There are stories of Ra carved into columns and on tomb walls. There are wall paintings and records written on papyrus. None of these—not one—reveals the secret name of Ra. It remained a secret between the sun god and the mistress of magic.

Now that Isis had what she wanted, she immediately cured Ra of the snake bite. But Ra was more than just revived. He was returned to his former glory. He shone as he had in the beginning. He was at his mightiest and most powerful once again.

The gods and goddesses rejoiced at Ra's rejuvenation and praised Isis for her skill at curing him. She knew that it would be dangerous to claim mastery over him. The others would turn against her, and she had no wish for that. No, she would use the knowledge wisely and would use the name when she needed help most. If she ever needed anything of Ra, he would have to give it to her.

Ra, well again and as young and as vibrant as at the beginning of time, climbed back aboard the *Boat of Millions of Years* and resumed his journey across the sky.

Satisfied that her well-laid plans had succeeded, Isis watched the sun god depart. She knew that one day she would use Ra's secret name to help her son, Horus. Isis would make sure that in the future Horus would become as powerful as Ra himself.

MYTHS AND LEGENDS RESOURCES

Here is just a sampling of other resources to look for. These resources on myths and legends are broken down into groups. Enjoy!

GENERAL MYTHOLOGY

The Children's Dictionary of Mythology *edited by David Leeming* (Franklin Watts, 1999). This volume is a dictionary of terms, names, and places in the mythology of various cultures around the world.

Creation Read-aloud Stories from Many Lands *retold by Ann Pilling* (Candlewick Press, 1997). This is a collection of sixteen stories retold in an easy style and presented in three general groups: beginnings, warmth and light, and animals.

The Crystal Pool: Myths and Legends of the World *by Geraldine McCaughrean* (Margaret K. McElderry Books, 1998). Twenty-eight myths and legends from around the world comprise this book. They include the Chinese legend "The Alchemist" and the Celtic legend "Culloch and the Big Pig."

Encyclopedia Mythica
http://www.pantheon.org/areas/mythology/
From this page of the *Encyclopedia Mythica* site you can select from any of five countries to have the mythology of that area displayed.

A Family Treasury of Myths from Around the World *retold by Viviane Koenig* (Abrams, 1998). This collection of ten stories includes myths from Egypt, Africa, Greece, and other places around the world.

Goddesses, Heroes and Shamans: The Young People's Guide to World Mythology *edited by Cynthia O'Neill and others* (Kingfisher, 1994). This book introduces the reader to over five hundred mythological characters from around the world.

Gods, Goddesses and Monsters: An Encyclopedia of World Mythology *retold by Sheila Keenan* (Scholastic, 2000). This beautifully illustrated book discusses the characters and themes of the myths of peoples from Asia to Africa, to North and South America.

The Golden Hoard: Myths and Legends of the World *retold by Geraldine McCaughrean* (Margaret K. McElderry Books, 1995). This book contains twenty-two myths and legends that are exciting, adventurous, magical, and poetic.

The Illustrated Book of Myths: Tales and Legends of the World *retold by Neil Philips* (Dorling Kindersley, 1995). This beautifully illustrated collection brings together many of the most popular of the Greek and Roman, Norse, Celtic, Egyptian, Native American, African, and Indian myths.

Kids Zone: Myths and Fables from Around the World
http://www.afroam.org/children/myths/myths.html
Just click on your choice of the sixteen stories listed, and it will appear in full text.

Legends http://www.planetozkids.com/oban/legends.htm
From this Web page you can get the full text of any of the many listings.

Mythical Birds and Beasts from Many Lands *retold by Margaret Mayo* (Dutton, 1996). This book is a collection of stories that illustrate the special powers of birds and beasts that have become a part of folklore around the world.

Mythology *by Neil Philip* (Alfred A. Knopf, 1999). This superbly illustrated volume from the "Eyewitness Books" series surveys the treatment of such topics as gods and goddesses, the heavens, creation, the elements, and evil as expressed in various mythologies around the world.

Mythology *CD-ROM for Mac and Windows* (Thomas S. Klise, 1996). Educational games and puzzles, a glossary, and a testing section are all part of this CD introduction to Greek and Roman mythology.

Myths and Legends *by Neil Philip* (DK Publishing, 1999). More than fifty myths and legends from around the world are explained through works of art, text, and annotation by one of the world's foremost experts on mythology and folklore.

**The New York Public Library Amazing Mythology:
A Book of Answers for Kids** by *Brendan January*
(John Wiley, 2000). Over two hundred questions and
answers introduce myths from many ancient cultures,
including Egyptian, Greek, Roman, Celtic, Norse, and
Native American.

Plays from Mythology: Grades 4-6 by *L.E. McCullough*
(Smith and Kraus, 1998). Twelve original plays are
included, each with suggestions for staging and costumes.

Sources for Mythology
http://www.best.com/~atta/mythsrcs.html
In addition to defining mythology and distinguishing
it from legend and folklore, this Web site lists primary
sources for myths from many regions of the world,
as well as magazines, dictionaries, and other resources
relating to mythology.

Sun, Moon and Stars *retold by Mary Hoffman*
(Dutton, 1998). More than twenty myths and legends
from around the world, all explaining what was seen
in the sky, make up this exquisitely illustrated book.

AFRICAN

African Gods and their Associates
http://www3.sympatico.ca/untangle/africang.html
This Web page gives you a list of the African gods
with links to further information about them.

African Myths
http://www.cybercomm.net/~grandpa/africanmyths.html
Full text of several tales from the Kenya, Hausa, Ashanti,
and Nyanja tribes are included in this Web site.

Anansi and the Talking Melon *retold by Eric A. Kimmel*
(Holiday House, 1994). Anansi, a legendary character
from Africa, tricks Elephant and some other animals into
thinking that the melon in which he is hiding can talk.

Children's Stories from Africa *4 Video recordings (VHS)*
(Monterey Home Video, 1997). Among the African
Legends on this page: "How the Hare Got His Long
Legs," "How the Porcupine Got His Quills," "The Brave
Sititunga," and "The Greedy Spider."

**The Hero with an African Face: Mythic Wisdom
of Traditional Africa** by *Clyde W. Ford* (Bantam, 2000).
"The Hero with an African Face" is only one of the
several stories included in this book, which also includes
a map of the peoples and myths of Africa and a
pronunciation guide for African words.

Kings, Gods and Spirits from African Mythology
retold by Jan Knappert (Peter Bedrick Books, 1993). This
illustrated collection contains myths and legends of the
peoples of Africa.

Legends of Africa by *Mwizenge Tembo* (Metro Books,
1996). This indexed and illustrated volume is from the
"Myths of the World" series.

Myths and Legends *retold by O. B. Duane* (Brockhampton
Press, 1998). Duane has vividly retold some of the most
gripping African tales.

CELTIC

Celtic Myths *retold by Sam McBratney* (Peter Bedrick,
1997). This collection of fifteen illustrated stories draws
from English, Irish, Scottish, and Welsh folklore.

Excalibur *retold by Hudson Talbott* (Books of Wonder,
1996). In this illustrated story from the legends of King
Arthur, Arthur receives his magical sword, Excalibur

Irish Fairy Tales and Legends *retold by Una Leavy*
(Robert Rinehart, 1996). Cuchulainn, Deirdre, and
Fionn Mac Cumhail are only three of the legendary
characters you will meet in this volume.

Irish Myths and Legends
http://www.mc.maricopa.edu/users/shoemaker/
   Celtic/index.html
This Web site is for those more serious in their
study of Irish myths and legends.

King Arthur by *Rosalind Kerven* (DK Publishing, 1998).
This book from the "Eyewitness Classic" series is a
retelling of the boy who was fated to be the "Once and
Future King" It includes illustrated notes to explain the
historical background of the story.

Robin Hood and His Merry Men *retold by Jane Louise*
Curry (Margaret K. McElderry, 1994). This collection
contains seven short stories of the legendary hero
Robin Hood, who lived with his band of followers in
Sherwood Forest.

**The World of King Arthur and his Court: People,
Places, Legend and Love** by *Kevin Crossley-Holland*
(Dutton, 1998). The author combines legend, anecdote,
fact, and speculation to help answer some of the questions regarding King Arthur and his chivalrous world.

CHINESE

Asian Mythology by *Rachel Storm* (Lorenz, 2000).
Included in this volume are myths and legends of China.

Chinese Culture
http://chineseculture.about.com/culture/
   chineseculture/msub82.htm
Use this Web page as a starting point for further
exploration about Chinese myths and legends.

Chinese Mythology by *Anne Birrell* (Johns Hopkins, 1999). This comprehensive introduction to Chinese mythology will meet the needs of the more serious and the general reader

Chinese Myths and Legends *retold by O. B. Duane and others* (Brockhampton Press, 1998). Introductory notes by the author give further explanation of the thirty-eight stories included in this illustrated volume.

Dragons and Demons by *Stewart Ross* (Cooper Beech, 1998). Included in this collection of myths and legends from Asia are the Chinese myths "Chang Lung the Dragon" and "The Ugly Scholar."

Dragons, Gods and Spirits from Chinese Mythology *retold by Tao Tao Liu Sanders* (Peter Bedrick Books, 1994). The stories in this book include ancient myths about nature, the gods, and creation as well as religious legends.

Fa Mulan: The Story of a Woman Warrior *retold by Robert D. San Souci* (Hyperion, 1998). Artists Jean and Mou-Sien Tseng illustrate this Chinese legend of a young heroine who is courageous, selfless, and wise.

Land of the Dragon: Chinese Myth by *Tony Allan* (Time-Life, 1999). This volume from the "Myth and Mankind" series includes many of China's myths as well as examination of the myth and its historical roots.

Selected Chinese Myths and Fantasies
http://www.chinavista.com/experience/story/story.html
From this Web site and its links you will find several Chinese myths that are enjoyed by children as well as the history of Chinese mythology.

EGYPTIAN

Egyptian Gods and Goddesses by *Henry Barker* (Grosset and Dunlap, 1999). In this book designed for the young reader, religious beliefs of ancient Egypt are discussed, as well as their gods and goddesses.

Egyptian Mythology A-Z: A Young Reader's Companion by *Pat Remler* (Facts on File, 2000). Alphabetically arranged, this resource defines words relating to Egyptian mythology.

Egyptian Myths *retold by Jacqueline Morley* (Peter Bedrick Books, 1999). Legends of the pharaohs, myths about creation, and the search for the secret of all knowledge, make up this illustrated book.

The Gods and Goddesses of Ancient Egypt by *Leonard Everett Fisher* (Holiday House, 1997). This artist/writer describes thirteen of the most important Egyptian gods.

Gods and Myths of Ancient Egypt by *Mary Barnett* (Regency House, 1996). Beautiful color photographs are used to further explain the text in this summary of Egyptian mythology.

Gods and Pharaohs from Egyptian Mythology *retold by Geraldine Harris* (Peter Bedrick Books, 1992). The author gives some background information about the Ancient Egyptians and then retells more than twenty of their myths.

Myth Man's Egyptian Homework Help
http://egyptmyth.com/
Cool Facts and Fun for Kids and *Egyptian Myth Encyclopedia* are only two of the many wonderful links this page will lead you to.

Myths and Civilizations of the Ancient Egyptians by *Sarah Quie* (Peter Bedrick Books, 1998). The author intersperses Egypt's myths with a history of its civilization in this illustrated volume.

The Secret Name of Ra *retold by Anne Rowe* (Rigby Interactive Library, 1996). In this Egyptian myth, Isis tricks Ra into revealing his secret name so that she and her husband Osiris can become rulers of the earth.

Tales from Ancient Egypt *retold by George Hart* (Hoopoe Books, 1994). The seven tales in this collection include stories of animals, of Isis and Horus, of a sailor lost on a magic island, and of pharaohs and their magicians.

Who's Who in Egyptian Mythology by *Anthony S. Mercatante* (Scarecrow Press, 1995). The author has compiled a concise, easy-to-use dictionary of ancient Egyptian deities.

GREEK

Allta and the Queen: A Tale of Ancient Greece by *Priscilla Galloway* (Annick Press, 1995). This made-up story, which is based on Homer's epic poem, *The Odyssey*, reads like a novel.

Cupid and Psyche *retold by M. Charlotte Craft* (Morrow Junior Books, 1996). This classic love story from Greek mythology will appeal to young and old.

Gods and Goddesses by *John Malam* (Peter Bedrick Books, 1999). This volume is packed with information about the important gods and goddesses of ancient Greece, including Zeus, Hera, Athena, and Hades.

Greek and Roman Mythology by *Dan Nardo* (Lucent, 1998). The author examines the historical development of Greco-Roman mythology, its heroes, and its influence on the history of Western civilization.

Guide for Using D'Aulaires' Book of Greek Myths in the Classroom by *Cynthia Ross* (Teacher Created Materials, 1993). This reproducible book includes sample plans, author information, vocabulary-building ideas, cross-curricular activities, quizzes, and many ideas for extending this classic work.

Hercules by *Robert Burleigh* (Harcourt Brace, 1999). Watercolor and color pencil illustrations help to tell the story of Hercules's final labor in which he went back to the underworld and brought back the three-headed dog, Cerberus.

Medusa by *Deborah Nourse Lattimire* (Joanna Cotler Books, 2000). The author/illustrator of this book re-creates the tragedy of one of the best-known Greek myths, the tale of the beautiful Medussa whose conceit causes a curse be placed on her.

The Myths and Legends of Ancient Greece *CD-ROM for Mac and Windows* (Clearvue, 1996). This CD conveys the heroic ideals and spirit of Greek mythology as it follows ten of the best-known myths.

Mythweb http://www.mythweb.com/ This Web page provides links to Greek gods, heroes, an encyclopedia of mythology, and teacher resources.

Pegasus, the Flying Horse *retold by Jane Yolen* (Dutton, 1998). This Greek myth tells of how Bellerophon, with the help of Athena, tames the winged horse Pegasus and conquers the monstrous Chimaera.

The Race of the Golden Apples *retold by Claire Martin* (Dial, 1991). Caldecott Medal winners Leo and Diane Dillon have illustrated this myth of Atalanta, the beautiful Greek princess.

The Random House Book of Greek Myths by *Joan D. Vinge* (Random House, 1999). The author retells some of the famous Greek myths about gods, goddesses, humans, heroes, and monsters, explaining the background of the tales and why these tales have survived.

The Robber Baby: Stories from the Greek Myths *retold by Anne Rockwell* (Greenwillow Books, 1994). Anne Rockwell, a well-known name in children's literature, has put together a superbly retold collection of myths that will be enjoyed by readers of all ages.

NORSE

Beowulf by *Welwyn Wilton Katz* (Groundwood, 2000). The illustrations in this classic legend are based on the art of the Vikings.

Favorite Norse Myths *retold by Mary Pope Osborne* (Scholastic, 1996). These fourteen tales of Norse gods, goddesses, and giants are based on the oldest written sources of Norse mythology, *Prose Edda* and *Poetic Edda*.

The Giant King by *Rosalind Kerven* (NTC Publishing Group, 1998). Photos of artifacts from the Viking Age illustrate these two stories that are rooted in Norse mythology.

Gods and Heroes from Viking Mythology by *Brian Branston* (Peter Bedrick Books, 1994). This illustrated volume tells the stories of Thor, Balder, King Gylfi, and other Nordic gods and goddesses

Handbook of Norse Mythology by *John Lindow* (Ambcc, 2001). For the advanced reader, this handbook covers the tales, their literary and oral sources, includes an A-to-Z of the key mythological figures, concepts and events, and so much more.

Kids Domain Fact File http://www.kidsdomain.co.uk/teachers/resources/ fact_file_viking_gods_and_goddesses.html This child-centered Web page is a dictionary of Viking gods and goddesses.

Myths and Civilization of the Vikings by *Hazel Martell* (Peter Bedrick, 1998). Each of the nine stories in this book is followed by a non-fiction spread with information about Viking society.

Norse Mythology: The Myths and Legends of the Nordic Gods *retold by Arthur Cotterell* (Lorenz Books, 2000). This encyclopedia of the Nordic peoples' myths and legends is generously illustrated with fine art paintings of the classic stories.

Odins' Family: Myths of the Vikings *retold by Neil Philip* (Orchard Books, 1996). This collection of stories of Odin, the All-father, and the other Viking gods Thor, Tyr, Frigg, and Loer is full of excitement that encompasses both tragedy and comedy.

Stolen Thunder: A Norse Myth *retold by Shirley Climo* (Houghton Mifflin, 1994). This story, beautifully illustrated by Alexander Koshkin, retells the Norse myth about the god of Thunder and the recovery of his magic hammer Mjolnir, from the Frost Giany, Thrym.

North American

Buffalo Dance: A Blackfoot Legend *retold by Nancy Can Laan* (Little, Brown and Company, 1993). This illustrated version of the Native North American legend tells of the ritual performed before the buffalo hunt.

The Favorite Uncle Remus *by Joel Chandler Harris* (Houghton Mifflin, 1948). This classic work of literature is a collection of stories about Brer Rabbit, Brer Fox, Brer Tarrypin, and others that were told to the author as he grew up in the South.

Iktomi Loses his Eyes: A Plains Indian Story *retold by Paul Goble* (Orchard Books, 1999). The legendary character Iktomi finds himself in a predicament after losing his eyes when he misuses a magical trick.

The Legend of John Henry *retold by Terry Small* (Doubleday, 1994). This African American legendary character, a steel driver on the railroad, pits his strength and speed against the new steam engine hammer that is putting men out of jobs.

The Legend of the White Buffalo Woman *retold by Paul Goble* (National Geographic Society, 1998). This Native American Plains legend tells the story of the White Buffalo Woman who gave her people the Sacred Calf Pipe so that people would pray and commune with the Great Spirit.

Myths and Legends for American Indian Youth
http://www.kstrom.net/isk/stories/myths.html
Stories from Native Americans across the United States are included in these pages.

Snail Girl Brings Water: a Navajo Story *retold by Geri Keams* (Rising Moon, 1998). This retelling of a traditional Navajo re-creation myth explains how water came to earth.

The Woman Who Fell from the Sky: The Iroquois Story of Creation *retold by John Bierhirst* (William Morrow, 1993). This myth describes how the creation of the world was begun by a woman who fell down to earth from the sky country, and how it was finished by her two sons.

South American (including Central American)

Gods and Goddesses of the Ancient Maya *by Leonard Everett Fisher* (Holiday House, 1999). With text and illustration inspired by the art, glyphs, and sculpture of the ancient Maya, this artist and author describes twelve of the most important Maya gods.

How Music Came to the World: An Ancient Mexican Myth *retold by Hal Ober* (Houghton Mifflin, 1994). This illustrated book, which includes author notes and a pronunciation guide, is an Aztec pourquoi story that explains how music came to the world.

Llama and the Great Flood *retold by Ellen Alexander* (Thomas Y. Crowell, 1989). In this illustrated retelling of the Peruvian myth about the Great Flood, a llama warns his master of the coming destruction and leads him and his family to refuge on a high peak in the Andes.

The Legend of the Poinsettia *retold by Tomie dePaola* (G. P. Putnam's Sons,1994). This beautifully illustrated Mexican legend tells of how the poinsettia came to be when a young girl offered her gift to the Christ child.

Lost Realms of Gold: South American Myth *edited by Tony Allan* (Time-Life Books, 2000). This volume, which captures the South American mythmakers' fascination with magic, includes the tale of the first Inca who built the city of Cuzco, as well as the story of the sky people who discovered the rain forest.

People of Corn: A Mayan Story *retold by Mary-Joan Gerson* (Little, Brown, 1995). In this richly illustrated creation story, the gods first try and fail, then try and fail again before they finally succeed.

Tales from the Rain Forest: Myths and Legends from the Amazonian Indians of Brazil *retold by Mercedes Dorson* (Ecco Press, 1997). Ten stories from this region include "The Origin of Rain" and "How the Stars Came to Be."

WHO'S WHO IN MYTHS AND LEGENDS

This is a cumulative listing of some important characters found in all eight volumes of the *World Book Myths and Legends* series.

A

Aegir (EE jihr), also called Hler, was the god of the sea and the husband of Ran in Norse myths. He was lord of the undersea world where drowned sailors spent their days.

Amma (ahm mah) was the creator of the world in the myths of the Dogon people of Africa. Mother Earth was his wife, and Water and Light were his children. Amma also created the people of the world.

Amun (AH muhn), later Amun-Ra, became the king of gods in later Egyptian myths. Still later he was seen as another form of Ra.

Anubis (uh NOO bihs) in ancient Egypt was the god of the dead and helper to Osiris. He had the head of a jackal.

Ao (ow) was a giant turtle in a Chinese myth. He saved the life of Kui.

Aphrodite (af ruh DY tee) in ancient Greece was the goddess of love. She was known for her beauty. The Romans called her Venus.

Arianrod (air YAN rohd) in Welsh legends was the mother of the hero Llew.

Arthur (AHR thur) in ancient Britain was the king of the Britons. He probably was a real person who ruled long before the age of knights in armor. His queen was Guinevere.

Athena (uh THEE nuh) in ancient Greece was the goddess of war. The Romans called her Minerva.

Atum (AH tuhm) was the creator god of ancient Egypt and the father of Shu and Tefnut. He later became Ra-Atum.

B

Babe (bayb) in North American myths was the big blue ox owned by Paul Bunyan.

Balder (BAWL dur) was the god of light in Norse myths. He was the most handsome of all gods and was Frigga's favorite son.

Balor (BAL awr) was an ancient chieftain in Celtic myths who had an evil eye. He fought Lug, the High King of Ireland.

Ban Hu (bahn hoo) was the dog god in a myth that tells how the Year of the Dog in the Chinese calendar got its name.

Bastet (BAS teht), sometimes Bast (bast) in ancient Egypt was the mother goddess. She was often shown as a cat. Bastet was the daughter of Ra and the sister of Hathor and Sekhmet.

Bellerophon (buh LEHR uh fahn) in ancient Greek myths was a hero who captured and rode the winged horse, Pegasus.

Blodeuwedd was the wife of Llew in Welsh legends. She was made of flowers woven together by magic.

Botoque (boh toh kay) in Kayapó myths was the boy who first ate cooked meat and told people about fire.

Brer Rabbit (brair RAB iht) was a clever trickster rabbit in North American myths.

C

Chameleon (kuh MEEL yuhn) in a Yoruba myth of Africa was a messenger sent to trick the god Olokun and teach him a lesson.

Conchobar (KAHN koh bahr), also called Conor, was the king of Ulster. He was a villain in many Irish myths.

Coyote (ky OH tee) was an evil god in myths of the Maidu and some other Native American people.

Crow (kroh) in Inuit myths was the wise bird who brought daylight to the Inuit people.

Cuchulain (koo KUHL ihn), also Cuchullain or Cuchulan, in Irish myths was Ireland's greatest warrior of all time. He was the son of Lug and Dechtire.

Culan (KOO luhn) in Irish myths was a blacksmith. His hound was killed by Setanta, who later became Cuchulain.

D

Davy Crockett (DAY vee KRAHK iht) was a real person. He is remembered as an American frontier hero who died in battle and also in legends as a great hunter and woodsman.

Dechtire (DEHK teer) in Irish myths was the sister of King Conchobar and mother of Cuchulain.

Deirdre (DAIR dray) in Irish myths was the daughter of Fedlimid. She refused to wed Conchobar. It was said that she would lead to Ireland's ruin.

Di Jun (dee joon) was god of the Eastern Sky in Chinese myths. He lived in a giant mulberry tree.

Di Zang Wang (dee zahng wahng) in Chinese myths was a Buddhist monk who was given that name when he became the lord of the underworld. His helper was Yan Wang, god of the dead.

Dionysus (dy uh NY suhs) was the god of wine in ancient Greek myths. He carried a staff wrapped in vines.

Dolapo was the wife of Kigbo in a Yoruba myth of Africa.

E

Eight Immortals (ihm MAWR tuhlz) in Chinese myths were eight ordinary human beings whose good deeds led them to truth and enlightenment. The Eight Immortals were godlike heroes. They had special powers to help people.

El Niño (ehl NEEN yoh) in Inca myths was the ruler of the wind, the weather, and the ocean and its creatures.

Emer (AYV ur) in Irish myths was the daughter of Forgal the Wily and wife of Cuchulain.

F

Fafnir (FAHV nihr) in Norse myths was a son of Hreidmar. He killed his father for his treasure, sent his brother Regin away, and turned himself into a dragon.

Frey (fray), also called Freyr, was the god of summer in Norse myths. His chariot was pulled by a huge wild boar.

Freya (FRAY uh) was the goddess of beauty and love in Norse myths. Her chariot was pulled by two large cats.

Frigga (FRIHG uh), also called Frigg, in Norse myths was the wife of Odin and mother of many gods. She was the most powerful goddess in Asgard.

Frog was an animal prince in an Alur myth of Africa. He and his brother, Lizard, competed for the right to inherit the throne of their father.

Fu Xi (foo shee) in a Chinese myth was a boy who, with his sister Nü Wa, freed the Thunder God and was rewarded. His name means Gourd Boy.

G

Gaunab was Death, who took on a human form in a Khoi myth of Africa. Tsui'goab fought with Gaunab to save his people.

Geb (gehb) in ancient Egypt was the Earth itself. All plants and trees grew from his back. He was the brother and husband of Nut and the father of the gods Osiris, Isis, Seth, and Nephthys.

Glooscap (glohs kap) was a brave and cunning god in the myths of Algonquian Native American people. He was a trickster who sometimes got tricked.

Guinevere (GWIHN uh vihr) in British and Welsh legends was King Arthur's queen, who was also loved by Sir Lancelot.

Gwydion (GWIHD ih uhn) in Welsh legends was the father of Llew and the nephew of the magician and ruler, Math.

H

Hades (HAY deez) in ancient Greece was the god of the dead. Hades was also called Pluto (PLOO toh). The Romans called him Dis.

Hairy Man was a frightening monster in African American folk tales.

Harpy (HAHRP ee) was one of the hideous winged women in Greek myths. The hero Jason and his Argonauts freed King Phineas from the harpies' power.

Hathor (HATH awr) was worshiped in the form of a cow in ancient Egypt, but she also appeared as an angry lioness. She was the daughter of Ra and the sister of Bastet and Sekhmet.

Heimdall (HAYM dahl) was the god in Norse myths who guarded the rainbow bridge joining Asgard, the home of the gods, to other worlds.

Hel (hehl), also called Hela, was the goddess of death in Norse myths. The lower half of her body was like a rotting corpse. Hel was Loki's daughter.

Helen (HEHL uhn), called Helen of Troy, was a real person in ancient Greece. According to legend, she was known as the most beautiful woman in the world. Her capture by Paris led to the Trojan War.

Heng E (huhng ay), sometimes called Chang E, was a woman in Chinese myths who became the moon goddess. She was the wife of Yi the Archer.

Hera (HEHR uh) in ancient Greece was the queen of heaven and the wife of Zeus. The Romans called her Juno.

Heracles (HEHR uh kleez) in ancient Greek myths was a hero of great strength. He was the son of Zeus. He had to complete twelve tremendous tasks in order to become one of the gods. The Romans called him Hercules.

Hermes (HUR meez) was the messenger of the gods in Greek myths. He wore winged sandals. The Romans called him Mercury.

Hoder (HOO dur) was Balder's twin brother in Norse myths. He was blind. It was said that after a mighty battle he and Balder would be born again.

Hoenir (HAY nihr), also called Honir, was a god in Norse myths. In some early myths, he is said to be Odin's brother.

Horus (HAWR uhs) in ancient Egypt was the son of Isis and Osiris. He was often shown with the head of a falcon. Horus fought Seth to rule Egypt.

Hreidmar (HRAYD mahr) was a dwarf king in Norse myths who held Odin for a huge pile of treasure. His sons were Otter, Fafnir, and Regin.

Hyrrokkin (HEER rahk kihn) in Norse myths was a terrifying female giant who rode an enormous wolf using poisonous snakes for reins.

I

Irin-Mage (eereen mah geh) in Tupinambá myths was the only person to be saved when the creator, Monan, destroyed the other humans. Irin-Mage became the ancestor of all people living today.

Isis (EYE sihs) in ancient Egypt was the goddess of fertility and a master of magic. She became the most powerful of all the gods and goddesses. She was the sister and wife of Osiris and mother of Horus.

J

Jade Emperor (jayd EHM puhr uhr) in Buddhist myths of China was the chief god in Heaven.

Jason (JAY suhn) was a hero in Greek myths. His ship was the Argo, and the men who sailed with him on his adventures were called the Argonauts.

Johnny Appleseed (AP uhl seed) was a real person, John Chapman. He is remembered in legends as the person who traveled across North America, planting apple orchards.

K

Kaboi (kah boy) was a very wise man in a Carajá myth. He helped his people find their way from their underground home to the surface of the earth.

Kewawkwuí (kay wow kwoo) were a group of powerful, frightening giants and magicians in the myths of Algonquian Native American people.

Kigbo (keeg boh) was a stubborn man in a Yoruba myth of Africa. His stubbornness got him into trouble with spirits.

Kodoyanpe (koh doh yahn pay) was a good god in the myths of the Maidu and some other Native American people. He was the brother of the evil god Coyote.

Kuang Zi Lian (kwahng dsee lee ehn) in a Taoist myth of China was a very rich, greedy farmer who was punished by one of the Eight Immortals.

Kui in Chinese myths was an ugly, brilliant scholar who became God of Examinations.

Kvasir (KVAH sihr) in Norse myths was the wisest of all the gods in Asgard.

L

Lancelot (lan suh laht) in British and Welsh legends was King Arthur's friend and greatest knight. He was secretly in love with Guinevere.

Lao Zi (low dzuh) was the man who founded the Chinese religion of Taoism. He wrote down the Taoist beliefs in a book, the *Tao Te Ching*.

Li Xuan (lee shwahn) was one of the Eight Immortals in ancient Chinese myths.

Light (lyt) was a child of Amma, the creator of the world, in a myth of the Dogon people of Africa.

Lizard (LIHZ urd) was an animal prince in an Alur myth of Africa. He was certain that he, and not his brother, Frog, would inherit the throne of their father.

Llew Llaw Gyffes (LE yoo HLA yoo GUHF ehs), also Lleu Law Gyffes, was a hero in Welsh myths who had many adventures. His mother was Arianrod and his father was Gwydion.

Loki (LOH kee) in Norse myths was a master trickster. His friends were Odin and Thor. Loki was half giant and half god, and could be funny and also cruel. He caused the death of Balder.

Lord of Heaven was the chief god in some ancient Chinese myths.

Lug (luk) in Irish myths was the Immortal High King of Ireland, Master of All Arts.

M

Maira-Monan (mah ee rah moh nahn) was the most powerful son of Irin-Mage in Tupinambá myths. He was destroyed by people who were afraid of his powers.

Manco Capac (mahn kih kah pahk) in Inca myths was the founder of the Inca people. He was one of four brothers and four sisters who led the Inca to their homeland.

Manitou (MAN ih toh) was the greatest and most powerful of all gods in Native American myths of the Iroquois people.

Math (mohth) in Welsh myths was a magician who ruled the Welsh kingdom of Gwynedd.

Michabo (mee chah boh) in the myths of Algonquian Native American people was the Great Hare, who taught people to hunt and brought them luck. He was a son of West Wind.

Monan (moh nahn) was the creator in Tupinambá myths.

Monkey (MUNG kee) is the hero of many Chinese stories. The most cunning of all monkeys, he became the king of monkeys and caused great troubles for the gods.

N

Nanook (na NOOK) was the white bear in myths of the Inuit people.

Naoise (NEE see) in Irish myths was Conchobar's nephew and the lover of Deirdre. He was the son of Usnech and brother of Ardan and Ainle.

Nekumonta (neh koo mohn tah) in Native American myths of the Iroquois people was a person whose goodness helped him save his people from a terrible sickness.

Nü Wa (nyuh wah) in a Chinese myth was a girl who, with her brother, Fu Xi, freed the Thunder God and was rewarded. Her name means Gourd Girl.

Nuada (NOO uh thuh) in Irish myths was King of the Tuatha Dé Danann, the rulers of all Ireland. He had a silver hand.

O

Odin (OH dihn), also called Woden, in Norse myths was the chief of all the gods and a brave warrior. He had only one eye. He was the husband of Frigga and father of many of the gods. His two advisers were the ravens Hugin and Munin.

Odysseus (oh DIHS ee uhs) was a Greek hero who fought in the Trojan War. The poet Homer wrote of his many adventures.

Oedipus (ED uh puhs) was a tragic hero in Greek myths. He unknowingly killed his own father and married his mother.

Olodumare (oh loh doo mah ray) was the supreme god in Yoruba myths of Africa.

Olokun (oh loh koon) was the god of water and giver of life in Yoruba myths of Africa. He challenged Olodumare for the right to rule.

Orpheus (AWR fee uhs) in Greek myths was famed for his music. He followed his wife, Euridice, to the kingdom of the dead to plead for her life.

Osiris (oh SY rihs) in ancient Egypt was the ruler of the dead in the kingdom of the West. He was the brother and husband of Isis and the father of Horus.

P

Pamola (pah moh lah) in the myths of Algonquian Native American people was an evil spirit of the night.

Pan Gu (pahn goo) in Chinese myths was the giant who was the first living being.

Pandora (pan DAWR uh) in ancient Greek myths was the first woman.

Paris (PAR ihs) was a real person, a hero from the city of Troy. He captured Helen, the queen of a Greek kingdom, and took her to Troy.

Paul Bunyan (pawl BUHN yuhn) was a tremendously strong giant lumberjack in North American myths.

Perseus (PUR see uhs) was a human hero in myths of ancient Greece. His most famous adventure was killing Medusa, a creature who turned anyone who looked at her to stone.

Poseidon (puh SY duhn) was the god of the sea in myths of ancient Greece. He carried a three-pronged spear called a trident to make storms and control the waves. The Romans called him Neptune.

Prometheus (pruh MEE thee uhs) was the cleverest of the gods in Greek myths. He was a friend to humankind.

Q

Queen Mother of the West was a goddess in Chinese myths.

R

Ra (rah), sometimes Re (ray), was the sun god of ancient Egypt. He was often shown with the head of a hawk. Re became the most important god. Other gods were sometimes combined with him and had Ra added to their names.

Ran (rahn) was the goddess of the sea in Norse myths. She pulled sailors from their boats in a large net and dragged them underwater.

Red Jacket in Chinese myths was an assistant to Wen Chang, the god of literature. His job was to help students who hadn't worked very hard.

S

Sekhmet (SEHK meht) in ancient Egypt was a blood-thirsty goddess with the head of a lioness. She was the daughter of Ra and the sister of Bastet and Hathor.

Setanta in Irish myths was Cuchulain's name before he killed the hound of Culan.

Seth (set), sometimes Set, in ancient Egypt was the god of chaos and confusion, who fought Horus to rule Egypt. He was the evil son of Geb and Nut.

Shanewis (shah nay wihs) in Native American myths of the Iroquois people was the wife of Nekumonta.

Shu (shoo) in ancient Egypt was the father of the sky goddess Nut. He held Nut above Geb, the Earth, to keep the two apart.

Sinchi Roca was the second emperor of the Inca. According to legend, he was the son of Ayar Manco (later known as Manco Capac) and his sister Mama Ocllo.

Skirnir (SKEER nihr) in Norse myths was a brave, faithful servant of the god Frey.

Sphinx (sfihngks) in Greek myths was a creature that was half lion and half woman, with eagle wings. It killed anyone who failed to answer its riddle.

T

Tefnut (TEHF noot) was the moon goddess in ancient Egypt. She was the sister and wife of Shu and the mother of Nut and Geb.

Theseus (THEE see uhs) was a human hero in myths of ancient Greece. He killed the Minotaur, a half-human, half-bull creature, and freed its victims.

Thor (thawr) was the god of thunder in Norse myths. He crossed the skies in a chariot pulled by goats and had a hammer, Mjollnir, and a belt, Meginjardir.

Thunder God (THUN dur gahd) in Chinese myths was the god of thunder and rain. He got his power from water and was powerless if he could not drink.

Tsui'goab (tsoo ee goh ahb) was the god of rain in myths of the Khoi people of Africa. He was a human who became a god after he fought to save his people.

Tupan (too pahn) was the spirit of thunder and lightning in Inca myths.

Tyr (tihr) was the god of war in Norse myths. He was the bravest god and was honorable and true, as well. He had just one hand.

U

Utgard-Loki (OOT gahrd LOH kee) in Norse myths was the clever, crafty giant king of Utgard. He once disguised himself as a giant called Skrymir to teach Thor a lesson.

W

Water God (WAW tur gahd) in Chinese myths was a god who sent rain and caused floods.

Wen Chang (wehn chuhng) in Chinese myths was the god of literature. His assistants were Kui and Red Jacket.

Wu (woo) was a lowly courtier in a Chinese myth who fell in love with a princess.

X

Xi He (shee heh) in Chinese myths was the goddess wife of Di Jun, the god of the eastern sky.

Xiwangmu (shee wahng moo) in Chinese myths was the owner of the Garden of Immortal Peaches.

Xuan Zang (shwahn dsahng), also called Tripitaka, was a real person, a Chinese Buddhist monk who traveled to India to gather copies of religious writings. Legends about him tell that Monkey was his traveling companion.

Y

Yan Wang (yahn wahng) was the god of the dead and judge of the first court of the Underworld in Chinese myths. He was helper to Di Zang Wang.

Yao (yow) was a virtuous emperor in Chinese myths. Because Yao lived simply and was a good leader, Yi the Archer was sent to help him.

Yi (yee) was an archer in Chinese myths who was sent by Di Jun to save the earth, in answer to Yao's prayers.

Z

Zeus (zoos) in ancient Greece was the king of gods and the god of thunder and lightning. The Romans called him Jupiter.

Zhao Shen Xiao (zhow shehn shi ow) in Chinese myths was a good magistrate, or official, who arrested the greedy merchant Kuang Zi Lian.

MYTHS AND LEGENDS GLOSSARY

This is a cumulative glossary of some important places and terms found in all eight volumes of the *World Book Myths and Legends* series.

A

Alfheim (AHLF hym) in Norse myth was the home of the light elves.

Asgard (AS gahrd) in Norse myths was the home of the warrior gods who were called the Aesir. It was connected to the earth by a rainbow bridge.

Augean (aw JEE uhn) stables were stables that the Greek hero Heracles had to clean as one of his twelve labors. He made the waters of two rivers flow through the stables and wash away the filth.

Avalon (AV uh lahn) in British legends was the island where King Arthur was carried after he died in battle. The legend says he will rise again to lead Britain.

B

Bard (bahrd) was a Celtic poet and singer in ancient times. A bard entertained people by making up and singing poems about brave deeds.

Battle of the Alamo (AL uh moh) was a battle between Texas settlers and Mexican forces when Texas was fighting for independence from Mexico. It took place at the Alamo, a fort in San Antonio, in 1836.

Bifrost (BEE fruhst) in Norse myths was a rainbow bridge that connected Asgard with the world of people.

Black Land in ancient Egypt was the area of fertile soil around the banks of the River Nile. Most people lived there.

Brer Rabbit (brair RAB iht) myths are African American stories about a rabbit who played tricks on his friends. The stories grew out of animal myths from Africa.

C

Canoe Mountain in a Maidu myth of North America was the mountain on which the evil Coyote took refuge from a flood sent to drown him.

Changeling (CHAYNG lihng) in Celtic myths was a fairy child who had been swapped with a human baby at birth. Changelings were usually lazy and clumsy.

Confucianism (kuhn FYOO shuhn IHZ uhm) is a Chinese way of life and religion. It is based on the teachings of Confucius, also known as Kong Fu Zi, and is more than 2,000 years old.

Creation myths

Creation myths (kree AY shuhn mihths) are myths that tell how the world began.

D

Dwarfs (dwawrfs) in Norse myths were small people of great power. They were skilled at making tools and weapons.

F

Fairies (FAIR eez) in Celtic myths were called the Little People. They are especially common in Irish legends, where they are called leprechauns.

Fomors (FOH wawrz) in Irish myths were hideous giants who invaded Ireland and were fought by Lug.

G

Giants (JY uhnts) in Norse myths were huge people who had great strength and great powers. They often struggled with the warrior gods of Asgard.

Gnome (nohm) was a small, odd-looking person in the myths of many civilizations. In Inca myths, for example, gnomes were tiny people with very big beards.

Golden Apples of the Hesperides (heh SPEHR uh deez) were apples of gold in a garden that only the Greek gods could enter. They were collected by the hero Heracles as one of his twelve labors.

Golden fleece was the fleece of a ram that the Greek hero Jason won after many adventures with his ship, Argo, and his companion sailors, the Argonauts.

Green Knoll (nohl) was the home of the Little People, or fairies, in Irish and Scottish myths.

J

Jotunheim (YUR toon hym) in Norse myths was the land of the giants.

L

Lion men in myths of Africa were humans who can turn themselves into lions.

Little People in Celtic legends and folk tales are fairies. They are often fine sword makers and blacksmiths.

M

Machu Picchu (MAH choo PEE choo) is the ruins of an ancient city built by the Inca in the Andes Mountains of Peru.

Medecolin (may day coh leen) were a tribe of evil sorcerers in the myths of Algonquian Native American people.

Medicine (MEHD uh sihn) **man** is a wise man or shaman who has special powers. Medicine men also appear as beings with special powers in myths of Africa and North and South America. Also see **Shaman.**

Midgard (MIHD gahrd) in Norse myths was the world of people.

Muspell (MOOS pehl) in Norse myths was part of the Underworld. It was a place of fire.

N

Nidavellir in Norse myths was the land of the dwarfs.

Niflheim in Norse myths was part of the Underworld. It included Hel, the kingdom of the dead.

Nirvana (nur VAH nuh) in the religion of Buddhism is a state of happiness that people find when they have freed themselves from wanting things. People who reach Nirvana no longer have to be reborn.

O

Oracle (AWRR uh kuhl) in ancient Greece was a sacred place served by people who could foretell the future. Greeks journeyed there to ask questions about their fortunes. Also see **Soothsayer.**

P

Pacariqtambo (pahk kah ree TAHM boh) in Inca myths was a place of three caves from which the first people stepped out into the world. It is also called Paccari Tampu.

Poppykettle was a clay kettle made for brewing poppy-seed tea. In an Inca myth, a poppykettle was used for a boat.

Prophecy (PRAH feh see) is a prediction made by someone who foretells the future.

R

Ragnarok (RAHG nah ruhk) in Norse myths was the final battle of good and evil, in which the giants would fight against the gods of Asgard.

S

Sahara (sah HAH rah) is a vast desert that covers much of northern Africa.

Seriema was a bird in a Carajá myth of South America whose call led the first people to try to find their way from underground to the surface of the earth.

Shaman (SHAH muhn) can be a real person, a medicine man or wise person who knows the secrets of nature. Shamans also appear as beings with special powers in some myths of North and South America. Also see **Medicine man.**

Soothsayer (sooth SAY ur) in ancient Greece was someone who could see into the future. Also see **Oracle.**

Svartalfheim (SVAHRT uhl hym) in Norse myths was the home of the dark elves.

T

Tar Baby was a sticky doll made of tar used to trap Brer Rabbit, a tricky rabbit in African American folk tales.

Tara (TAH rah) in Irish myths was the high seat, or ruling place, of the Irish kings.

Trickster (TRIHK stur) **animals** are clever ones that appear in many myths of North America, South America, and Africa.

Trojan horse. See Wooden horse of Troy.

Tuatha dÈ Danann (THOO uh huh day DUH nuhn) were the people of the goddess Danu. Later they were known as gods of Ireland themselves.

V

Vanaheim (VAH nah hym) in Norse myths was the home of the fertility gods.

W

Wadjet eye was a symbol used by the people of ancient Egypt. It stood for the eye of the gods Ra and Horus and was supposed to bring luck.

Wheel of Transmigration (tranz my GRAY shuhn) in the religion of Buddhism is the wheel people's souls reach after they die. From there they are sent back to earth to be born into a higher or lower life.

Wooden horse of Troy was a giant wooden horse built by the Greeks during the Trojan War. The Greeks hid soldiers in the horse's belly and left the horse for the Trojans to find.

Y

Yang (yang) is the male quality of light, sun, heat, and dryness in Chinese beliefs. Yang struggles with Yin for control of things.

Yatkot was a magical tree in an African myth of the Alur people.

Yggdrasil (IHG drah sihl) in Norse myths was a mighty tree that held all three worlds together and reached up into the stars.

Yin (yihn) is the female quality of shadow, moon, cold, and water in Chinese beliefs. Yin struggles with Yang for control of things.

CUMULATIVE INDEX

This is an alphabetical list of important topics covered in all eight volumes of the **World Book Myths and Legends** series. Next to each entry is at least one pair of numbers separated by a slash mark (/). For example, the entry for Argentina is "**Argentina 8/4**". The first number tells you what volume to look in for information. The second number tells you what page you should turn to in that volume. Sometimes a topic appears in more than one place. When it does, additional volume and page numbers are given. Here's a reminder of the volume numbers and titles: 1, *African Myths and Legends;* 2, *Ancient Egyptian Myths and Legends;* 3, *Ancient Greek Myths and Legends;* 4, *Celtic Myths and Legends;* 5, *Chinese Myths and Legends;* 6, *Norse Myths and Legends;* 7, *North American Myths and Legends;* 8, *South American Myths and Legends.*

For information on other World Book products, visit our Web site at www.worldbook.com or call 1-800-WORLDBK (967-5325).

For information on sales to schools and libraries, call 1-800-975-3250.

Cover background illustration by Paul Perreault

World Book, Inc.
233 North Michigan Avenue
Chicago, IL 60601

Pages 1–47: format and illustrations, ©1997 Belitha Press; text, ©1997 Philip Ardagh

Printed in Hong Kong
2 3 4 5 6 7 8 9 10 10 09 08 07 06 05 04 03 02

ISBN(set): 0-7166-2613-6
African Myths and Legends
ISBN: 0-7166-2605-5
LC: 2001026492

Ancient Egyptian Myths and Legends
ISBN: 0-7166-2606-3
LC: 2001026501

Ancient Greek Myths and Legends
ISBN: 0-7166-2607-1
LC: 2001035959

Celtic Myths and Legends
ISBN: 0-7166-2608-X
LC: 20011026496

Chinese Myths and Legends
ISBN: 0-7166-2609-8
LC: 2001026489

Norse Myths and Legends
ISBN: 0-7166-2610-1
LC: 2001026488

North American Myths and Legends
ISBN: 0-7166-2611-X
LC: 2001026490

South American Myths and Legends
ISBN: 0-7166-2612-8
LC: 2001026491